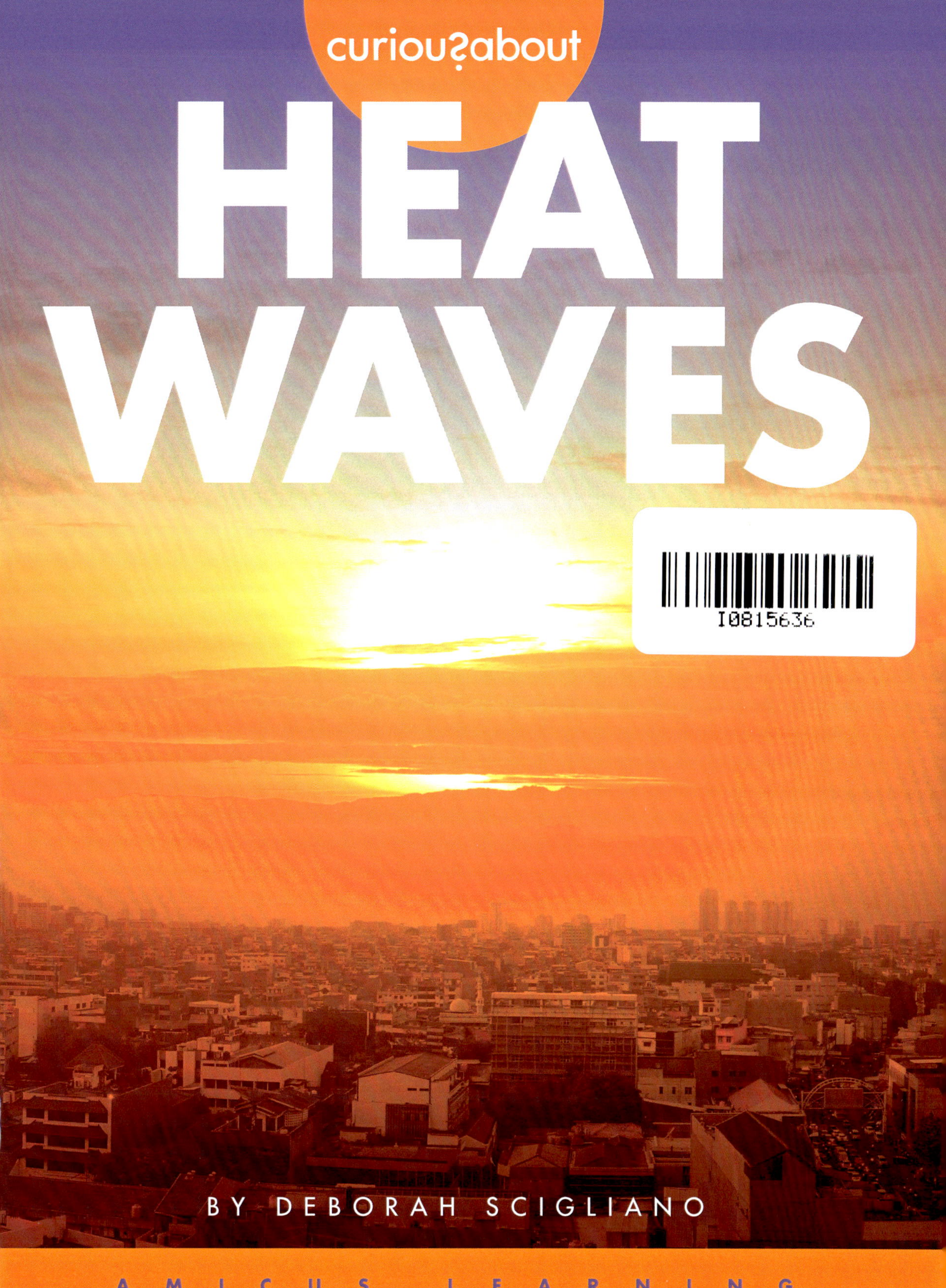

curious about

# HEAT WAVES

BY DEBORAH SCIGLIANO



AMICUS LEARNING

# What are you

# curious about?

Curious About is published by
Amicus Learning, an imprint of Amicus
P.O. Box 227, Mankato, MN 56002
www.amicuspublishing.us





Editor: Ana Brauer
Series Designer: Kathleen Petelinsek
Book Designer and Photo Researcher: Kathleen Petelinsek

Library of Congress Cataloging-in-Publication Data
Names: Scigliano, Deborah A., 1951– author
Title: Curious about heat waves / by Deborah Scigliano.
Description: Mankato, MN : Amicus Learning, an imprint of Amicus, [2026] | Series: Curious about extreme weather | Includes bibliographical references and index. | Audience: Ages 6–9 | Audience: Grades 2–3 | Summary: "Where do heat waves happen? Learn the causes and effects of one of nature's deadliest weather events in this question-and-answer book for elementary-aged readers. Includes infographics, table of contents, glossary, books and websites for further research, and index"— Provided by publisher.
Identifiers: LCCN 2025012821 (print) | LCCN 2025012822 (ebook) | ISBN 9798892008396 library binding | ISBN 9798892009058 paperback | ISBN 9798892009713 ebook
Subjects: LCSH: Heat waves (Meteorology)—Juvenile literature
Classification: LCC QC981.8.A5 S35 2026 (print) | LCC QC981.8.A5 (ebook)| DDC 551.5/253—dc23/eng/20250721
LC record available at https://lccn.loc.gov/2025012821
LC ebook record available at https://lccn.loc.gov/2025012822

Photo Credits: Alamy Stock Photo/Arthur Grace/ZUMA Press, 8, Xinhua, 9 (left); envato/Image-Source, 3, 16–17; Shutterstock/ANURAK PONGPATIMET, 2, 11, De Visu, 9 (right), J Dennis, 2, 6–7, Jaromir Chalabala, 20, Jessica2, 12, leolintang, cover, 1, Mariyana M, 16, maruco, 14–15, Maryia Blizniakova, 12–13, Melinda Nagy, 21, Muhammad Asfandyar bhatti, 22, 23, New Africa, 18–19, Nicholas J Klein, 5, PradeepGaurs, 9 (middle), Rotshild, 10

# CHAPTER ONE

# What happens during a heat wave?

Heat affects a lot of things. Crops can dry out. Wildfires can start and spread. People use more air conditioning. More electricity is used. This can cause a power outage. The heat can also make people and animals sick.

**DID YOU KNOW?**
**A heat wave is two or more days with unusually hot weather.**

During a heat wave, it's better to stay indoors.

# What causes a heat wave?

Los Angeles, California, often has heat waves in summer.

Air becomes trapped under high pressure. This stops the air from cooling. Sunny days and **humidity** add to the heat. Humidity is **water vapor** in the air. This makes the air feel hotter. The heat index shows how hot it feels with the humidity.

**DID YOU KNOW?**
**Heat waves kill more people than any other wild weather.**

## WORST HEAT WAVES

UNITED STATES

**1901**
Eastern United States
June–August
9,500 deaths

**1980**
Nationwide United States
June–September
1,700 deaths

# Where do heat waves happen?

They happen all over the world. Every continent except Antarctica has heat waves. They happen in deserts and cities. The buildings in cities keep heat a long time. This makes cities hotter than places around them.

# Are heat waves dangerous?

They can be! If it gets too hot, people can get heat exhaustion or heat stroke. Heat exhaustion can cause dizziness and nausea. Heat stroke can cause headaches and confusion. People with heat stroke can die quickly. Call emergency services.

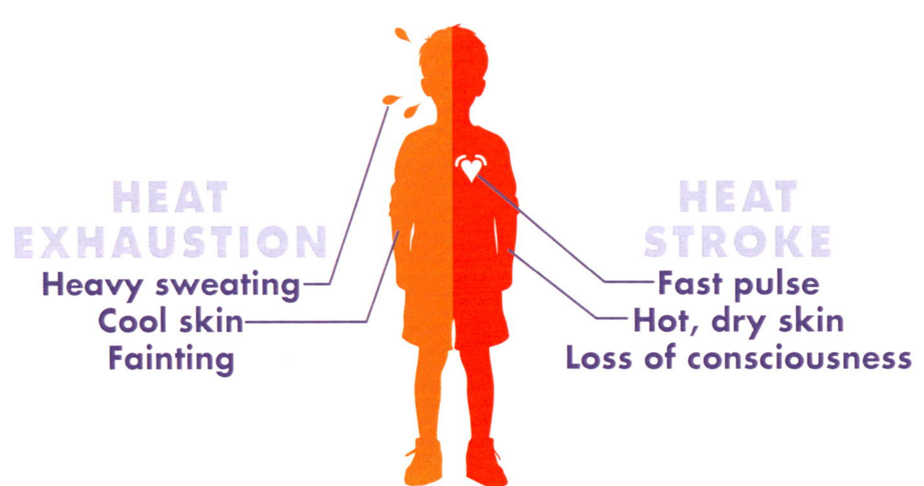

Stay safe by knowing when the heat is too much.

# Can I go outside in a heat wave?

SUN
SCREEN
SPF 35

Sunscreen helps protect your skin from the sun.

You can. But try to stay inside during the hottest times. Use sunscreen when you go outside. Wear loose light-colored clothing and a hat. Cotton is good to wear. Stay in the shade when possible. Be sure to take it slow. Save high-energy activities for when it is cooler.

Humidity makes us sweat more and feel hotter.

# Why is it so sticky in a heat wave?

High heat makes it harder for us to cool down. Usually, our sweat **evaporates** and cools us off. Sweat does not evaporate when the humidity is high. High humidity makes it harder to cool off. We feel sticky and hot.

# CHAPTER THREE

# What are good things to do in a heat wave?

Drink lots of water on hot days.

**Hydrate**! Drink plenty of water. Avoid sugary drinks and caffeine. Taking a trip to the pool can help you to stay cool and have fun. Reading in the air conditioning is great to do in a heat wave.

**Swimming is a fun way to beat the heat.**

# How can I keep cool?

Stay in air conditioning when you can. No air conditioning? You can use fans. No power? You and your family can find a place to go to cool down. Eat light, cool meals like salads. Take a cool shower or bath.

Sitting in front of a fan can cool you down.

# How can I help my pets in a heat wave?

**Give your pets a lot of water when it's hot.**

Pets need to keep cool, too. Walk your dog in the morning or evening. Stay out of the strong heat during the mid-day. The sidewalk can get very hot. This can hurt your dog's paws. Make sure to give your pets lots of cool, clear water. Let them chill out in the heat of the day.

Splashing in a lake helps dogs cool off on hot days.

## ASK MORE QUESTIONS

**How much water do I need each day?**

**How can we save electricity during a heat wave?**

**Try a BIG QUESTION: How does climate change affect heat waves?**

## SEARCH FOR ANSWERS

**Search the library catalog or the Internet.**
A librarian, teacher, or parent can help you.

**Using Keywords**
Find the looking glass.

**Keywords are the most important words in your question.**

**If you want to know about:**

- how much water you need, type: WATER INTAKE BY AGE
- saving electricity when it's hot, type: SAVING POWER IN A HEAT WAVE

# LEARN MORE

## FIND GOOD SOURCES

**Here are some good, safe sources you can use in your research.**
Your librarian can help you find more.

### Books

**All about Heat Waves and Droughts: Discovering Earth's Scorching Weather**
by Steve Tomecek, 2021.

**Heat Wave**
by Lauren Redniss, 2024.

### Internet Sites

**Kiddle: Heat Wave facts for kids**
*https://kids.kiddle.co/Heat_wave*
Kiddle is an online encyclopedia for kids. Learn more about heat waves.

**Real Simple: 50 Fun Indoor Activities and Things to Do on a Hot Day**
*https://www.realsimple.com/health/mind-mood/heat-wave-activities*
Find out about activities that you can do when it's too hot outside.

Every effort has been made to ensure that these websites are appropriate for children. However, because of the nature of the Internet, it's impossible to guarantee that these sites will remain active indefinitely or that their contents will not be altered.

## SHARE AND TAKE ACTION

**Try a heat experiment.**
Find a sidewalk with grass nearby. Feel the air right above a sidewalk and then above grass. How does the air feel?

**Work with an adult you know to plant more trees and plants**.
They help to make places cooler.

**Be sure to stay hydrated!**
Help your family and friends to learn how much water they should drink each day.

# GLOSSARY

**evaporate** To pass off or cause to pass off into vapor from a liquid state.

**humidity** The amount of moisture in the air.

**hydrate** To make your body take in water or other liquid.

**unusual** Differing from what happens most of the time.

**water vapor** Water as a gas, especially when below boiling temperature and spread through the atmosphere.

# INDEX



## About the Author

Deborah Scigliano is an educator and a writer. She has taught elementary students and college students. She loves to write for children. Science, especially weather, is a special interest of hers.